RICKEY MARSH

UNLOCK GRATITUDE

The Ultimate Guide to Living Your Life With Gratitude,
Discover How You Can Achieve Greatness
By Using The Power of Gratitude

Descrierea CIP a Bibliotecii Naţionale a României
RICKEY MARSH
   UNLOCK GRATITUDE. The Ultimate Guide to Living Your Life With Gratitude, Discover How You Can Achieve Greatness By Using The Power of Gratitude / Rickey Marsh. – Bucharest: Editura My Ebook, 2020
   ISBN 978-606-983-593-7

RICKEY MARSH

UNLOCK GRATITUDE

The Ultimate Guide to Living Your Life With Gratitude, Discover How You Can Achieve Greatness By Using The Power of Gratitude

My Ebook Publishing House
Bucharest, 2020

TABLE OF CONTENTS

INTRODUCTION

Author, William Arthur Ward, once said, "Gratitude can transform common days into thanksgivings, turn routine jobs into joy, and change ordinary opportunities into blessings." Gratitude is the unique quality of being entirely thankful for what you have, as well as always being ready to appreciate and help others.

Gratitude is one of the primary keys to living a happy and prosperous life. For when you show gratitude for what you have, you are content with your life and positive about all that it has to offer.

If you feel a lack of gratitude in your life and are afraid that it may be creating a void, it is time for you to take action and learn how you can develop gratitude to live a happier life. If you are currently in a difficult situation in your life and think that it is impossible for you to be thankful, then it's time you learned how to cultivate gratitude and achieve greatness. With your determination and effort, you can quickly develop a sense of gratitude and become content with yourself and your life.

You can learn about what gratitude is and all the benefits it can bring you in your life. If you're ready to improve your overall well- being and live a happier life, then you can learn to cultivate gratitude and achieve greatness. Gratitude, like any skill, can be learned and you can develop habits of gratitude. With practice, gratitude can become a choice. You can learn how to bring gratitude into your life and improve your relationships.

CHAPTER 1

DEFINING GRATITUDE

Almost every day, we say thanks. We absentmindedly tell it to the grocery store checkout clerk and to the barista at our local coffee shop but are these sincere expressions of gratitude, or merely a response we've been conditioned to give?

What exactly is gratitude?

Is it something different than saying "thanks," or is the "thanks" a component of gratitude?

As you will discover as you read through this guide, a simple "thanks" can have a powerful impact on both the person communicating their appreciation and the person receiving that appreciation. This is especially true when the genuine emotion of gratitude backs the word. The question then becomes, what exactly is gratitude?

The Roman philosopher, Cicero, described gratitude as the greatest of virtues and the parent of all others. It is the key that opens all doors and is the quality that makes us and keeps us young. This statement, spoken more than two thousand years ago, is quite compelling. It speaks of gratitude as a virtue or quality of being. Gratitude is just this and so much more. Gratitude is also an emotion. It is something that we feel deep in our hearts. We can feel it toward others, when people are grateful to us, or when we see a person express gratitude toward another. As a sentiment or as an exchange between people, there is simplicity to being grateful. And yet, when trying to understand this simplicity, we can find a more complex meaning. Gratitude is an emotion, it is an experience, and it is a conscious choice for awareness.

Connections in your relationships are both strengthened and fostered with gratitude.

At its core, gratitude holds an experience of universal belonging. We can experience a real sense of overall well-being when you practice the intentional cultivation of gratitude in our lives.

Gratitude as a State of Being

Take a moment and shut your eyes and try to recall a time when you felt appreciated. Remember this event as if it were happening at this very moment.

What words did you hear?

What did your body feel like at that moment? What triggered the experience?

What were you thinking at the moment?

What did you enjoy most about being appreciated?

What about this particular moment brought you to remember it today?

Write down your answers to these questions in a notebook that you can refer back to later.

There isn't a single definition of gratitude. Gratitude has been conceptualized and defined in the context of attitudes, emotions, morals, traits, habits, and even coping techniques. Gratitude is without a doubt, an incredibly complex and dynamic emotion. It is a skill that contributes to the satisfaction in relationships and human excellence.

Gratitude as an Emotion

In this context, we need to be sure to distinguish emotion from the mood. Emotion is about something or someone. It is about a personally significant circumstance or experience. A mood, on the other hand, is not connected to any object and is not dependent on any one thing. By exploring gratitude in this way, we can see that it occurs in response to an action within the framework of a relationship. Something has been given by someone and received by someone else. This exchange helps to foster the emotion of gratitude.

Gratitude is an empathic emotion, which means that in order to experience the emotion in exchange, the receiver needs to place himself in the position of the giver. A feeling of

14

gratitude in response to the gift requires the recipient of the gift to sense the giver's positive intention. It is this recognition and empathic connection that provides the foundation for the emotional experience of gratitude in the interaction.

We can express gratitude for any number of reasons. We can be grateful for receiving personal benefits, such as advice from a mentor, or we can be grateful for material items, like a gift, our home, or a car. Gratitude can also be fostered through interpersonal fulfillment, such as getting a hug from a friend. Or, we can experience gratitude for a monetary gain, like getting a raise at work.

CHAPTER 2

FINDING GRATITUDE IN SOCIETY

When we look at the United States today, many see a rich and powerful nation that is admired. It is not respected so much for its military might and technological advancements, but for the freedoms that its citizens enjoy, which enable them to strive to achieve their dreams.

The founding values of the nation are what laid the template for everyone who came after the bloody war for independence. The United States and what it is today was shaped by wave after wave of immigrants who adopted our values, putting the country on its path of progress.

While the initial years were tough for these new immigrants, they learned to adapt, and survived the first few bleak winters.

Realizing that hard work was the only way to forge ahead and succeed in their new lives, the learned to express gratitude for what they had been given in their new home of opportunity.

It was this gratitude for the simple gifts they received, like a roof over their heads and food on the table, which allowed them to progress in the best possible way.

As proven by those that came before us, gratitude can play a seminal role in shaping your destiny and your life.

Gratitude in Today's Time

In today's highly consumerist society, where quarterly growth figures have become a measure of a nation's standing or where possessing a killer instinct is considered a great asset, the question then becomes whether or not gratitude has a place in our society.

While we are all still pursuing happiness, our ways of finding it varies. For some, we try to obtain it through service and charity, while others try to find it in esoteric books and at the feet of gurus. Unfortunately, for the majority of us, we try to find happiness through material acquisition. This has turned the society into one that feels it is entitled to all it receives and obtains, and shuns the idea of expressing gratitude for all that we have. Things are now viewed, by many, through the prism of sales and purchase, and some even view both relationships and possessions from a use- and-discard perspective.

Thankfully, gratitude is just as contagious as materialism. As soon as you realize that gratitude can help you reach the happiness and greatness you've been chasing.

CHAPTER 3

USING GRATITUDE IN YOUR RELATIONSHIPS

It is easy to get caught up in the hectic routine of everyday living and forget to express our appreciation to those that matter to us the most. Take a moment to think about the relationships in your life and consider a time when you felt gratitude for that person.

One of the most common mistakes we can make in our relationships is the assumption error. This occurs when we assume that someone in our life knows what we are thinking or feeling, or when we believe that someone else should know what we are thinking or feeling. The problem with this is that if we don't let those people in our lives that are important to us know that they matter, they don't know that they matter.

For most of us, we have stopped being consciously aware in our lives. We have turned on the autopilot and are merely drifting through life. Our brains and body have become so familiar with our routine that we put little thought or attention into our daily lives. Our minds are usually busy making lists, recalling events of the day, or thinking ahead, that we've stopped being consciously aware. We tend to go through the emotions that we know so well and miss out on all the nuances of the experience in the process.

Communicating Gratitude

Having an increasing awareness of gratitude can have a ripple effect throughout your relationships. There is evidence that when we share our gratitude, whether, in kindness, words, or gifts, we nurture our relationships, helping them to grow stronger and closer. Knowing this, it makes perfect sense that we need to explore how we can convey our appreciation to those that matter the most to us.

While there is nothing wrong with expressing your gratitude by saying, "thanks a lot," or "nice work," these expressions of gratitude are often taken for granted and seldom convey the message as powerfully as we want. One way you can verbally to express your appreciation in a manner that will foster connection in your relationships is by including three things in your expression: (1) observation, (2) feeling, and (3) need.

In sharing your observation, you just state what you observe, like holding the door open, washing the dishes, or taking out the trash. These everyday actions do make a difference, but they often go unacknowledged. Sometimes just letting someone know that you noticed can make a world of difference to that person. Next, you need to let that person know that what they did have a positive impact on you.

The final aspect of communicating gratitude is often times the trickiest. It can be difficult to acknowledge that we need others, but we do. It is important to remember that we don't exist in little bubbles and that we are consistently affected by those around us. Letting someone know that they were there when you needed them is an open doorway to establishing a connection with others.

When it comes to thinking about your own relationships and opportunities for gratitude, don't limit your expressions of gratitude to the things that people give you or do for you.

Sometimes it is just as valuable to share your appreciation for who they are as a person. Let the people in your life know that you not only appreciate what they do for you by who they are as well. Take the time to comment on someone's generosity, thoughtfulness, compassion, or just being who they are, and see how much happier you become in your relationships.

CHAPTER 4

THE POWER OF POSITIVE EMOTIONS
AND GRATITUDE

Wanting to be happy isn't an unrealistic desire. However, we seem to be misinformed about what happiness is. At times, we may think that we can find happiness in a new computer, a new shirt, or a new car. Other times, we may believe that indulging our impulses will make us happy. While these things in and of themselves aren't bad, you need to consider if any of these things have brought you true, lasting happiness.

A study of twins has demonstrated that approximately 50 percent of happiness levels are based on genetics. This means that there is some predisposition to happiness, but that also means that half of our happiness isn't wired into our DNA. Another study determined that 10 percent of our happiness is determined by our life circumstances like wealth, relationship status, health, etc. This means that if 50 percent of our happiness can be attributed to genetic makeup and 10 percent to circumstances, that leaves 40 percent of our happiness up to us and our behavior.

This 40 percent means that we have a significant say in how happy we are in our lives. It's not all up to chance, or someone else's whims or intentions. We have a choice. So what does this have to do with gratitude? Well, it turns out that research has shown that grateful people are indeed happier people. Gratitude can reduce the frequency and duration of depressive episodes, which makes a lot of sense because it is hard to feel bitterness, anger, envy, hostility, and resentment when you are feeling grateful. By its nature gratitude has the capability to block more negative and unpleasant emotions. When it comes to gratitude, it is essential for you to realize that the feelings you experience are valuable and that they all serve a purpose.

When you feel afraid, you may become anxious. This emotion puts your body in a state of alertness, so you're ready for anything and can grow in tune with our surroundings. Feeling anxious when you are walking down a poorly lit street at night, is an appropriate emotion and can help keep you safe. That same feeling of anxiety prior to speaking publicly can
24

prompt you to prepare for the event, and help you to have an excellent presentation ready to go.

Emotions that are typically referred to as negative are merely more unpleasant to experience. Bitterness, sadness, guilt, regret, shame, envy, resentment, and anxiety are not necessarily bad, but they can be uncomfortable to experience, especially if they feel that you often have. Your mind is somewhat programmed to focus on these emotions and give them more of your attention. This is because these are essential emotions in that they give you valuable information about yourself and how you are responding to your environment. Without these emotions, you wouldn't know if there was danger lurking around the corner, or if you are viewing something that is opposed to your moral and ethical views. These particular emotions can prompt you into taking action. The downside to these specific emotions is that you can quickly get stuck there, and you can begin to find yourself living in uncomfortable places.

Gratitude and other positive emotions don't discount the negative experience but can help you keep things in perspective and keep you from getting stuck in those negative emotions. Practicing gratitude is one way to transform your experiences toward more positive emotions and improving your relationships. If you work with appreciation, you will begin to shift your experience toward the positive.

Benefits of Gratitude

Gratitude has also been proven to increase our capacity for experiencing other positive emotions. Often, gratitude is described with the same feelings connected to it, like love, compassion, humility, comfort, passion, and confidence.

Cultivating gratitude can be a direct way to enhance these other emotions in your life.

Another benefit of gratitude that has been supported by several studies is that grateful people are more resilient and resistant to stress. When you can find the ability to be thankful for the things you have in your life, you find yourself able to move through challenges and difficulties in your lifetime and time again.

Gratitude helps us see our strength, open our hearts, and experience the fullness in our lives.

The good news is, you don't have to go through a crisis in order to find gratitude. Gratitude is an opportunity that is there waiting for you every day.

Gratitude can be learned. With practice, gratitude can be a choice, an intentional way of viewing the world. This is not to say that you should discount or make light of difficulties or painful experiences in your life, but you should choose not to let yourself become overwhelmed in these times, and find a way to see beyond them.

You can look with gratitude at what you learn about others and yourself when you're moving through hardships.

CHAPTER 5

MINDFULNESS, MEDITATION, AND GRATITUDE

It's amazing how often we adopt someone else's emotional story as our own. When we hear it and witness it often enough, we will begin to fall into those exact same patterns. Whether it's a habit and pattern of complaining, or of doing things a specific way, to some degree we all pick up on the habits and behaviors of those closest to us. While this isn't necessarily a bad thing, it is something that we can benefit from being more aware of. If we don't know that we're doing something, or why we are doing it, it can be difficult to tell if it is effective for us or how it may affect our relationships and experiences.

How can we recognize these patterns and "borrowed" patterns? How do we move from the less effective patterns and move to cultivate an attitude of gratitude? There are many ways that you can progress toward this, but to build awareness, the best path is through mindfulness practice. The simplest and the clearest definition of mindfulness is nothing more than "paying attention on purpose." Intentionally bringing your attention and your focus to the details and the experience of one chosen thing. You can be mindful of anything, your breath, the food you eat, or even vacuuming the floor. Being mindful merely is, noticing the experience of something as it is happening at the moment.

Practicing mindfulness can help to treat and prevent depression. Taking the time to focus your attention intentionally can change the imbalance of the chemical circuitry in your brain and help you to shift out of your negative thought patterns. Other research has discovered that mindful awareness practices can enhance the body's general functioning and promote healing, immune response, stress reactivity, and provide you with a general sense of physical well-being. You will also be able to improve your relationship with others when you practice mindfulness because it allows you to be better able to recognize nonverbal signals from others, but also acknowledge our part in the interaction.

Because our lives can get quite busy and hectic, we tend to go on autopilot and miss opportunities for connection and gratitude.

Sometimes, we even miss what we are experiencing at the moment. Taking a few minutes every day to stop, slow down, settle our bodies, and actually pay attention to the moments can have a profound impact on how we feel about the day and what we did to fill it.

Mindful Living Day-to-Day

Our thoughts, emotions, and behaviors are all connected. Each one feeds into the others and shapes our experiences with others and the world in which we live.

Practicing mindfulness helps us notice our experiences, our relationships, and our environment in a different context. With mindfulness practice, we can pay attention to our thoughts, behaviors, and emotions without judgment. When we are mindful, we begin to see our world and notice all the opportunities for gratitude that exist. Any daily routine, task, or errand can become an opportunity to practice mindfulness and gratitude. You can practice mindful gratitude anywhere at any time.

Mindfulness Practice Through Meditation

If you are struggling to incorporate mindfulness into your daily life, you can use meditation to train your brain to do it automatically. Mindfulness can be cultivated through mindfulness meditation, which is a systematic method for focusing your attention. You can learn to meditate on your own, following instructions in books or through the help of videos and tapes.

Some types of meditation involve, primarily, concentration, like repeating a phrase or focusing on the sensation of breathing. This concentration allows the constant flow of thoughts that inevitably arise to come and go. Concentration meditation techniques, as well as other activities, can induce a relaxation response, which can help to reduce your body's response to stress.

Getting Started with Mindfulness Meditation

Mindfulness meditation builds upon concentration practices. Once you establish concentration, you begin to observe the flow of your inner thoughts, emotions, and bodily sensations without judging them as either good or bad.

Then you start to open your mind and notice the external sensations around you such as sights, sounds, and touch that make up your moment-to-moment experience. The challenge in mindfulness meditation is to not latch onto any one particular idea, sensation, or emotion, or get caught up in thinking about the past or future. Instead, you should be watching what comes and goes in your mind to discover which mental habits produce a feeling of well-being or ones of suffering.

There are going to be times when you don't feel as though this process is at all relaxing. However, over time it will provide you a greater key to happiness and self-awareness as you become more and more comfortable with a broader range of experiences.

Practicing Gratitude Mediation

Gratitude meditation is one of the most influential and rewarding exercises you can do. When you're able to develop an attitude of gratitude you can start feeling more contented with your life and accomplish true happiness. Gratitude can make you feel good, and meditation will help you to achieve a deep state of relaxation and contemplation.

Gratitude meditation can be incorporated together, or you can spend a few minutes at the beginning of your meditation session taking deep breaths while you think of all the things that you are grateful for in your life.

You can start your gratitude mediation practice by taking a few moments to do some deep breathing relaxation techniques. Start by breathing in through your nose. This will extend your abdomen and cause your diaphragm to pull air into the bottom of your lungs, which will provide your body with a healthy dose of oxygen, and helping you to become more relaxed.

When you're ready, sit in a comfortable chair, one that is suitable for meditation, and close your eyes. Allow your muscles to begin to relax. Let go of your thoughts. When you feel relaxed and comfortable start to think about everything that you are grateful for in your life. The more that you are grateful for, the more you'll receive in your life. Whether you choose to practice gratitude meditation or gratitude relaxation and breathing on a regular basis the happier and healthier, you'll be.

CHAPTER 6

UNBALANCED GRATITUDE

So far, you've discovered that gratitude has a number of positive attributes and benefits. You've learned that people who are grateful tend to be happier, healthier, and are more satisfied in and with their relationships. Gratitude opens us up to being able to connect with others and can help us through stressful situations and experiences. However, it is essential to understand that every light casts a shadow, and gratitude is no exception. It is entirely possible to experience, or at least express, something similar to gratitude without the benefits.

In order for gratitude to occur in your relationships, there has to be an exchange from one to another. There has to be a giver and a receiver, and there has to be an awareness of that exchange. When the awareness of the gift is not present, the exchange becomes unbalanced. This can result in either a missed opportunity for gratitude or even a false expression of gratitude.

Unbalanced gratitude, or unhealthy appreciation, occurs when there is a sense that one should be grateful, but the feeling isn't there. It's the thought of, "I know I should be grateful, but I can't help but feel (guilty, awkward, suspicious, resentful) or some other variation of a feeling of unease.

Superficial Gratitude

Superficial gratitude is one that is not genuine or from the heart. It occurs most frequently when there is public expectation or demand for acknowledgment. The best example of this is the yearly award shows that are aired on television. The words of gratitude are present, but the sentiment behind those words is non-existent.

The challenge with this kind of gratitude is that it seldom makes you feel good. It doesn't come with the added benefits of the other emotions that are so often associated with gratitude; emotions of joy, happiness, love, connection, and even hope. Instead, superficial expressions of gratitude are often associated with a feeling of anxiety and resentment.

You can also end up with superficial gratitude when there are too many people to thank, more for the reason of not wanting to exclude anyone. When there is a long list of thanks being recited without the connection to what is being acknowledged, the sense of appreciation becomes diluted and has less meaning. There are many situations where you may feel pressured to offer thanks, even when you aren't feeling the emotion, which can lead you to another form of false gratitude.

Obligatory Gratitude

Obligatory gratitude shares some similarities with superficial gratitude. There ends up being an overwhelming sense of "should" behind the expression of thanks, rather than a genuine feeling of appreciation. This kind of gratitude often occurs when you feel a need to say "thanks" for a kindness that was received, but one that wasn't wanted or needed. You may feel obligatory gratitude when you feel obligated to thank someone for a gift that you neither wanted or like, or when someone is doing something for you that you want to do on your own.

Reestablishing Balance

Everyone, at one time or another, has experienced unbalanced gratitude. The critical thing to understand is that it is not true gratitude. Whether the false gratitude is stemming from cultural expectations or an intention to be perceived as better than another, it is missing the essential elements of the components that are necessary for gratitude to blossom in your life. If you find yourself engaged in an exchange of unbalanced gratitude, it is up to you to look for ways to restore the balance.

CHAPTER 7

HOW GRATITUDE EMPOWERS

On a psychological level, practicing gratitude allows us to become happier, more positive, and more amenable to finding joy and pleasure in everything that we do. Showing gratitude for the things we have and those around us also has social advantages as well because we become more generous and compassionate in our dealing with the world.

Studies have shown that gratitude helps us on both psychological and physical levels. Physically, when we practice gratitude in our lives, it can help to boost our immunity levels, which in turn can lead to us living a more healthy and energetic life. This can help to reduce the likeliness that we will fall ill and allow us to live a more active life.

Gratitude can empower you to understand better that life is all about the moments lived rather than continually looking out for the good or bad moments. Gratitude teaches us to be grateful for all the moments that make up our lives.

For example, take the case of someone who has just been in a car accident that resulted in them being hospitalized with their leg in a cast. Now instead of moping about how they would have to say in the hospital for a couple of weeks, the person is grateful that their life was saved and could look forward to catching up on some reading and the latest TV shows.

Become More Optimistic

Gratitude can help you develop an optimistic and positive perspective about life, even with all of its ups and downs. Living life with gratitude will enable you to understand and appreciate that taking the rough with the unruffled patience is the key to your happiness, contentment, and peace. Instilling an attitude of gratitude in children from an early age will help them value the blessings they have, leading them away from the current plague of the sense of entitlement that affects so many today. It has become far too easy for children today to take what they have for granted.

This ingratitude ends up putting them on a path that is difficult for them to find peace and contentment, which could impact their ability to having meaningful relationships in their lives, both at work and at home.

Become More Thankful

The best thing about the empowering nature of gratitude is the fact that it makes you view your own self in a new light. The more thankful you are for everything that is good in your life, the less you will dwell on those aspects of your personal life that falls short. Gratitude will also make you a more empathetic person who can appreciate the achievements of others without feeling envious. This can free you up to focus on doing the things in your life that work for you.

Become More Energized

Among the many beautiful ways that gratitude can empower your life is the way that it ends up energizing your being. The very act of embracing the positive and letting go of the negative can make you view your life with hope and optimism, which provides you with enthusiasm to give your best in everything that you do.

Gratitude is like the sunshine that breaks through the window and illuminates the room when you open the curtains in the morning.

Anybody and everybody has a need for this vital catalyst that can bring exciting wonder into your life.

Find Meaning in Life

Life is more than the relentless pursuit of material possessions and achieving goals. Having a sense of gratitude for what we have and wishing the best for everyone else puts us on the path of self- realization, allowing you to have contentment as a constant part of your life, as well as enables you to reach out to those who may need your help.

Become More Sociable

People who practice gratitude have more positive energy and tend to be more popular because of their more pleasant and affable personality. This can help you make more friends and have a deeper, more meaningful connection within your relationships. In general, grateful people are more helpful, more social, more trusting, and more appreciative.

CHAPTER 8

HOW TO LEARN GRATITUDE

Thankfully, gratitude can be learned. With the right application of practice and discipline, you can master an attitude of gratitude in your life. The thing about gratitude is that it may not be all that challenging for most people to express when things are going well. However, the moment a crisis occurs or an unhappy situation arises, people don't see much reason to be grateful. Many would rather complain about their life. The thing about gratitude, however, is that it is nothing more than a state of mind. You can, if you want, find a reason to feel grateful even in the darkest of hours.

No matter how terrible things may seem to be, there is always something for you to be grateful for. The thing to remember is that we are all on this planet for a short period, and as long as we live and breathe, we have something to celebrate.

If things have gone wrong, you have to remember that they can also get better.

When you take some time to observe the way grateful people conduct themselves, you will start to notice some commonalities in their behavior.

They Have Realistic Expectations of Life

Life rarely happens in the way you expect. The best students in school don't necessarily do better in life. There are numerous instances where somebody less talented than you is able to land the job that you wanted, or who find more success than you. No one knows what sort of cards we will be dealt with in life. When you are prepared for the surprises that life will inevitably throw at you, you will always be able to find a silver lining and be grateful.

They Are Unconditionally Happy

When you put a prior condition on being happy you will likely never reach that happiness. If you covet a particular sports car, that's okay, but if you decide that you are going to be depressed until you get it, what would happen if it suddenly goes out of production?

People who readily show gratitude for whatever good they see in their lives, no matter how small it is, are those who find it rather easy to be happy. Unconditional gratitude is definitely one of the prerequisites for living a happy life.

They Accept That the Good Comes With the Bad

People that can appreciate that the good comes with the bad will find that their hearts are grateful for the good in life while realizing and understanding the fact that there will likely be a corresponding downside. They know that as they bask in the warm glow of the summer sun, that the bleak cold of winter is just around the corner. Conversely, if it is raining heavily, they know that it is just a matter of time before the sun will shine.

They Are Optimistic

People who find it easy to express gratitude for the smallest bit of happiness don't get fazed by the changes in life. They are eternal optimists who just need the slightest glimmer of hope to be happy and content. For them, tomorrow is another day.

CHAPTER 9

DEVELOPING GRATITUDE HABITS

Gratitude is something that we have endless opportunities to feel each day. The challenge becomes not getting caught in the negativity bias of our brain. The negativity bias is our tendency to focus our attention on the more uncomfortable emotions such as fear, anxiety, anger, and sorrow. While these emotions are essential for us to because they prompt us to pay attention to things that may be threatening or dangerous, we shouldn't live in them or let them be the ones that inform our entire life experiences.

With practice, you can develop new patterns of thinking and new ways to experience your life. Just like with a new diet or exercise, engaging in a new behavior for one hour, one day, or one week, will not create a long-term change, but regular practice can create a change that is sustainable. It can quickly become a habit.

Something that you do automatically.

No matter what your situation, there is always an opportunity for gratitude. Even the most frustrating experiences can offer you a chance to practice gratitude, but can also allow you to observe it and be influenced by its presence.

Developing Habits

Any new behavior or routine will take time to develop into a new habit. The first time you drive a car, everything is new and requires your full attention. When you begin a new fitness plan, it takes some effort and commitment. Over time, the newness becomes something that you just do. The process is seldom simple and often requires some support or encouragement.

Developing a habit of gratitude will require some attention and effort on your part. While shifting gratitude into a consistent practice does take effort, it is a worthwhile investment of your energy. Research has shown that in addition to increasing your awareness of the abundance already present in your life, practicing gratitude gives you a wide range of benefits including:

- Improved ability to manage daily stress
- Increased optimism about the future
- A heightened sense of community
- Increased resiliency to traumatic events
- A heightened sense of emotional well-being
- Increased physical activity
- Improved sleep
- Improved physical health
- Reduction in feelings of depression
- Reduction in feelings of anxiety
- Positive impact on both cardiovascular and immune functions

It is critical to remember that habits take time to develop. There may be days where you forget about gratitude altogether. That's alright. You can pick up the practice again the following day. Over time, the practice of gratitude will become more automatic. Just like learning anything new, you have to give yourself patience and time to develop gratitude habits. With continued practice, you will notice the rewards in your own life unfold.

Practicing Giving

Entitled is a word that is used to describe many children and adolescents today. Entitlement is one of the most significant obstacles to gratitude. When you believe that everything is owed to you, how can you feel grateful or genuinely appreciative? This belief of deserving creates a wall that blocks gratitude.

So, the question becomes how you can shift from an attitude of entitlement to one of gratitude? There are several of ways that you can accomplish this. First, you can start by adjusting your own attitude and model a grateful attitude in your home. You can also teach your children about gratitude and giving rather than about deserving and owing. The key to teaching gratitude is to engage in activities and interactions that are focused on sharing, giving, and connecting rather than doing something in order to get something back.

As much as we live in a world where we are conditioned to give thanks, often without awareness, we also live in an age of entitlement, where more and more, people are finding themselves disappointed because they are not receiving what they believe they deserve. Believing that the world owes you anything is a false premise and will only lead you to experience disappointment, strains in your relationships, and further resentment and frustration.

Writing Gratitude

As you look for ways to combat entitlement and foster gratitude in your life, you can look to the simple act of writing thank-you notes. Often, when people talk about writing thank you notes, they are taken back to when they were required to write obligatory thank you notes for graduations, birthdays, weddings. In these situations, the writing of thank you notes can feel a bit daunting and can quickly become overwhelming. With many of these situations, the gifts that are purchased are out of a social obligation, and the thank you notes are also written from a place of social responsibility. While this may not be representative of sincere gratitude, it is a positive step in moving toward developing gratitude habits, because it is a way to acknowledge gifts received.

With that, you can go a step further and move past obligatory gratitude and into reflective gratitude. Reflective gratitude happens when you are able to step back from a situation, recall the event, and re-experience the emotions that occurred during that moment or span of time. Often, we don't realize the benefit that we're receiving from someone until after we have had time to reflect.

Thank you notes have a positive effect on those who receive them. Taking the time to reflect on the relationships you have developed, and the gifts that those relationships offer you can move you from a place of resentment or victimization into feeling appreciative of the gifts that you have received. It can also provide you with the opportunity to reflect on how you have affected those around you.

CHAPTER 10

CULTIVATING GRATITUDE IN YOUR LIFE

Now is your chance to practice cultivating gratitude in your life. This can be done by yourself or with others. The trick is to practice. As with any new skill that you are learning, developing an attitude of gratitude is going to take time. By incorporating the following practices into your every day life, you will find that, over time, you will experience the world a little bit differently. You will begin to see opportunities hiding in the most obvious places. You will notice richness in your relationships, and you will start to feel more connected to those around you.

Not all of these practices will be comfortable for you, and some might even make you feel a bit silly doing them. That's alright. Keep trying them. Some of these exercises will resonate with you, while others may not. The key to cultivating gratitude and achieving greatness is to keep practicing until it becomes intuitive.

The first few practices are meditations. As discussed in Chapter 5, meditation and mindfulness are essential aspects to finding gratitude in your daily life. If you aren't familiar with the practice of meditation, these exercises may be a bit challenging. If your thoughts begin to wander, or your mind goes into judgment and questioning mode, that's alright, merely redirect your attention to the practice at hand. It is essential that you be gentle with yourself. There is no right or wrong way to do these exercises.

Gratitude Meditation Practice

You need to begin this practice by sitting quietly in a comfortable chair. If you are comfortable with shutting your eyes, do it. If not, you can merely soften your gaze to the floor approximately three feet in front of you.

Quiet your mind and gently bring your attention and focus to your breathing. Take a deep breath through your nose and breathe into your heart. Try to visualize your heart filled with a soft, radiating, violet light.

As you breathe in, visualize a soft, pink light filling your heart, gently combining with the violet light that fills the space in your chest cavity.

As you exhale through your mouth, visualize a soft blue light moving from the violet light, and up through your body as you gently expel your breath through your mouth.

With each in-breath, say gently to yourself, "I am filled with gratitude." With each out breath, say to yourself, "I offer gratitude to the universe."

Continue this cycle for four minutes. When you have completed the time, gently open your eyes, or raise them from the floor.

Gratitude Meditation Journal Practice

For this exercise, you'll need to purchase a notebook or journal to keep by your bedside.

Each evening, prior to going to sleep, sit quietly and bring your attention to your breath, keeping your head relaxed.

If you are comfortable, close your eyes or soften your gaze at a fixed point on the ground about four feet in front of you.

Take a few deep breaths, paying attention to the inhale and exhale.

Think through the events of your day. Visualize those events as they occurred, be sure to pay close attention to moments that contained acts of kindness, laughter, or beauty. As you notice these occurrences, pay attention to how your body feels. Pay attention to the sensations that you are feeling. What kind of thoughts arise in your mind?

When you've completed reviewing your day, gently bring your attention back to your breath. Open your eyes and write down the observations in the journal.

Gratitude Journal Practice

Start noticing the things that occur each day for which you are grateful. These things can be big or small; it doesn't matter. The magnitude of what you are identifying isn't essential, but instead that you are noticing things that you can appreciate about the day. You may be grateful for a person, for opportunities that were presented to you, for a good cup of coffee or tea, or perhaps that the day has come to a close and you are now preparing to lie in your bed and rest your head on your favorite pillow.

Every night, before you go to sleep, write down the things that you were grateful for throughout your day. Again, these can be big or small; it doesn't matter. Write down at least three things every day and once a week, sit down and review your journal entries.

Gratitude Breathing

Even in the busiest of days, there are small moments where you can practice gratitude. Take a moment, two or three times a day, to slow down and bring your full attention to your breathing.

Notice each breath. Observe every inhale and exhale, noticing that at that moment you don't have to do anything but breathe. Once your breath has your full attention, silently say the words "thank you" on each of the next five to eight exhalations as a gentle reminder that right now, at this moment, you're okay. These silent "thank yous" can serve as a quick reminder of the gift of your breath and how lucky you are to be alive.

Do this practice at least three times per week.

Gratitude Reminders

It is extremely easy to forget something, especially when you are trying to form a new habit. Placing visual reminders around your home or workspace can help you stay on track with your goals.

Create reminders that will prompt you throughout the day to think about gratitude, or merely to pause and reflect. Here are some ideas for your gratitude reminders.

Carry a small stone in your pocket. When you notice the rock, pause for a moment and reflect on gratitude.

Place a note on your office wall, refrigerator at home, or bathroom mirror that says, "I am grateful."

Set the alarm on your phone to go off one or more times a day as a cue to pause and reflect on gratitude.

Schedule a five-minute "gratitude break" in your office calendar two or three times each week. Use the calendar reminder feature to help keep you on track.

Have a "gratitude partner," someone with whom you check in daily to help identify aspects of gratitude in the day.

Family Gratitude Practice

You don't need to practice gratitude alone. Gratitude is, after all, about relationships and exchange. You can create an attitude of gratitude within your home as a family activity.

Keep a gratitude list for your family.

Place a whiteboard or sheet of paper on the refrigerator or some other easy-to-find location and have everyone in the family add to it daily. Things on the list can be big or small; it doesn't matter.

Choose one day a week to share the list together at a shared meal. Create a new list each week.

Gratitude Letter

There is always an opportunity for you to express your appreciation and gratitude, even if years have passed. Reflecting on those who have helped you in the past or present, and writing this down, can be a powerful means of cultivating gratitude.

Think of someone in your life for whom you feel grateful, but haven't yet thanked. Write a letter to this person expressing your appreciation for them. Let them know how they have affected your life. If possible, deliver the letter in person and read it to them before giving it to them.

Thank-you Notes

Like the gratitude letter, the thank-you note is a compelling expression of gratitude. It allows you, as the recipient, an opportunity to savor the gift/benefit, and allows the person who gave you something the opportunity to feel recognized and appreciated.

Keep a box of thank you notes around and get in the habit of writing thank you notes. Write them for the unexpected, for someone who said something kind to you or helped you out when you needed it.

CONCLUSION

Gratitude has the power to dramatically transform your life dramatically and is something that can be quickly learned. As you begin to notice the good that is surrounding your life and start to show gratitude for everything you have, you will begin to become happier and more content with your life. Gratitude will allow you to become more hopeful for the future and excited to see what life has in store for you.

Start practicing an attitude of gratitude and start a fresh life, making it an integral part of your every day and start benefiting both physically and mentally from the mighty act of gratitude.

Printed by Libri Plureos GmbH in Hamburg, Germany